10 in the Bed

a traditional song adapted by Charnan Simon
illustrated by Leslie Tryon

www.kindermusik.com

ISBN 1-58987-054-9

Published in 2004 by Kindermusik International, Inc.

Do-Re-Me & You! is a trademark of Kindermusik International, Inc.

Printed in China
First Printing, July 2004

Once upon a time, all the farmyard animals decided to have a sleepover.

There were 10 in the bed, and the little one said, . . .

So they all rolled over, and . . .

"Roll over! Roll over!" So they all rolled over, and . . .

"Roll over! Roll over!" So they all rolled over, and . . . .

"Roll over! Roll over!" So they all rolled over, and . . .

"Roll over! Roll over!" So they all rolled over, and . . .

"Roll over! Roll over!" So they all rolled over, and . . .

"Roll over! Roll over!" So they all rolled over, and . . .

"Roll over! Roll over!" So they all rolled over, and . . .

"Roll over! Roll over!" So they all rolled over, and . . .

. . . one fell out.

There was **1** in the bed, and the little one said, . . .

Ten in the Bed

traditional